Variations on a Gregorian Theme

For Organ

JENNIFER BATE

We hope you enjoy *Variations on a Gregorian Theme*.
Further copies of this and our many other books are available
from your local music shop or Christian bookshop.

In case of difficulty, please contact the publisher direct by writing to:

The Sales Department
KEVIN MAYHEW LTD
Buxhall
Stowmarket
Suffolk IP14 3BW

Phone 01449 737978
Fax 01449 737834
E-mail info@kevinmayhewltd.com

Please ask for our complete catalogue of outstanding
Organ Music.

First published in Great Britain in 2000 by Kevin Mayhew Ltd.

© Copyright 2000 Kevin Mayhew Ltd.

ISBN 1 84003 571 4
ISMN M 57004 704 8
Catalogue No: 1400246

0 1 2 3 4 5 6 7 8 9

The music in this book is protected by copyright and may not be reproduced in any way for sale
or private use without the consent of the copyright owner.

Front cover design: Jonathan Stroulger
Music setter: Kate Gallagher
Proof reader: Marian Hellen

Printed and bound in Great Britain

Composer's note

These variations are intended to be effective on virtually any instrument, from the most modest two-manual and pedal organ without aids to registration, to those of more sophisticated resources. The piece is written for the player of average ability, and following are some suggestions on registration and interpretation.

Variation 1 The canon should be played very flexibly, reflecting the free nature of plainsong. If two 4ft tones do not balance well, either hand can play on a quiet 8ft an octave higher.

Variation 2 This should be bold and bright, in sharp contrast to Variations 1 and 3. On larger instruments (or where the Oboe is too soft), the theme can be on a Trumpet, with proportionally louder accompaniment.

Variation 3 The shifting ostinato bass is meant to give this waltz a perverse limp! Although the main theme is in canon in the accompaniment, it should be overshadowed by the right-hand figuration, built from the 'Amen'.

Variation 4 In some buildings it may be advisable to adopt a slower tempo for clarity, both in the canon and the veiled chords.

Variation 5 On larger instruments this may be treated as a trio, with reeds and mixtures on both manuals, over a full pedal, uncoupled.

Variation 6 This movement draws on the harmonic language of Percy Whitlock, whose music I admire. He made a similar dedication to Delius at the head of his 'Carol' (No. 1 of Four Extemporisations). On instruments with no suitable 4ft pedal stop, couple a 4ft from the Great with Great to Pedal for the first canonic section. There is time after the second-time bar to adjust stops – if necessary, by hand – for the second canon. The theme, presented complete in the coda, should be clear but very serene.

Duration 6 minutes

JENNIFER BATE

To Helen Harris

VARIATIONS ON A GREGORIAN THEME

CONDITOR ALME SIDERUM

Jennifer Bate

(Vespers, 1st Sunday in Advent)

VARIATION 1 - MUSETTE

VARIATION 2 - COURANTE

VARIATION 3 - WALTZ

Sw. Flute 8', Salicional 8', Gemshorn 4'
Gt. Flutes 8' 4'
Ped. 16' 8'

© Copyright 2000 Kevin Mayhew Ltd.
It is illegal to photocopy music.

VARIATION 4 - ROMANCE

Sw. Celestes
Ped. Soft Reed 16' or Clear 16' 8'

Andante (♩ = 84)

© Copyright 2000 Kevin Mayhew Ltd.
It is illegal to photocopy music.

VARIATION 5 - MARCH

Gt. Diapasons 8' 4' 2', Mixture, Trumpet
Ped. Full + Reed 16'
Gt. to Ped.

VARIATION 6 - SARABANDE
Homage to Percy Whitlock